FUN FACTS
ABOUT BABIES

FUN FACTS

ABOUT BABIES

Written and illustrated by

Richard Torregrossa

A DELL TRADE PAPERBACK

A DELL TRADE PAPERBACK

Published by
Dell Publishing
a division of
Bantam Doubleday Dell Publishing Group, Inc.
1540 Broadway
New York, New York 10036

Library of Congress Cataloging in Publication Data

Torregrossa, Richard.
        Fun facts about babies / Richard Torregrossa.
            p.   cm.
        ISBN 0-440-50783-9
        1. Infants—Miscellanea.   I. Title.
    HQ774.T67 1997   97-9108
        305.232—dc21   CIP

Printed in the United States of America

Published simultaneously in Canada

Text design by Ellen Gleeson/Folio Graphics Co., Inc.

October 1997

10   9   8   7   6   5   4   3   2   1

FFG

To Grace Lile and Arthur S. Goldwag,
and Janet and Charles Keenan.
Their loving fascination with their babies
inspired this book.

Many, *many* thanks to Ken and Justine Wenman for their invaluable assistance with this book. I am extremely indebted to them for their patient editorial guidance and keen graphic-design contributions during this book's early stages.

Thanks also to: Alice Peck for taking an interest in this book when few others would. Art Goldwag, for his friendship, good humor, and support; my sister, Judith Wilson, for her encouragement; and all the people who sent me interesting facts and tidbits about babies.

I would also like to thank my editor, Mary Ellen O'Neill, for her cheerfulness, professionalism, and the care with which she guided this project along.

And, finally, a special thanks to attorney Nina Graybill for all of her efforts.

"Babies are such a nice way to start people."
—Don Harold

"If a child is to keep alive his inborn sense of wonder without any such gift from the faeries, he needs the companionship of at least one adult who can share it, rediscovering with him the joy, excitement, and mystery of the world we live in." —Rachel Carson

FUN FACTS
ABOUT BABIES

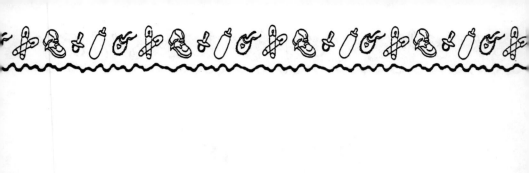

Think Your Baby Is Big?

The heaviest healthy baby born to a healthy mother was a boy weighing twenty-two pounds, eight ounces. He was born to Signora Carmelina Fedeli of Aversa, Italy, in September 1995.

Babies Are Ahead

The brain grows more during infancy than at any other time. It doubles its volume and reaches approximately 60 percent of its adult size in one year.

Shush! Baby's Asleep

Babies have shorter sleep cycles than adults. They are also lighter sleepers. According to experts, "sleeping through the night" is a mere five-hour stretch for most infants.

Most Popular Names
(IN THE UNITED STATES)

According to recent surveys, the most popular boy's name is Michael. And the most popular girl's name is Ashley, with Jessica coming in a close second. The next most popular names, in descending order, are as follows.

BOYS	GIRLS
Matthew	Sarah
James	Brittany
Zachary	Amanda
Joshua	Megan
Ryan	Elizabeth
Nicholas	Michelle
Nathan	Ann
Steven	Taylor
David	Kimberly

Reach Out and Touch Someone . . .

Especially your baby. New research shows that the gentle hug and touch of parents not only comforts baby but helps baby develop in other important ways.

For example, premature infants in a "grower nursery," where they're given special care to gain needed weight, achieved 74 percent more weight when they received extra touching, either from nurses or from parents. They were also healthier, with better digestion and enhanced neurological development. They were happier and better behaved, too, compared to babies who did not receive such attention.

Cry, Baby, Cry

A baby's long crying jags might make *you* want to cry, but experts say that it's a process more sophisticated and purposeful than we might at first suspect.

Baby's tears actually serve a dual function. Those produced by eye irritants have a different chemical composition than those produced because of crankiness or upset emotions. The former wash unwanted particles away with a saline solution, and the latter soothe the baby with antistress hormones.

Smells Like You, Mom

The sense of smell is actually quite developed in newborns, and in their mothers. According to William Sears, M.D., and Martha Sears, R.N., authors of *The Baby Book*, not only can a newborn distinguish Mother's voice from a stranger's, baby can also pick out her individual scent.

An interesting study of six-day-old newborns found that when Mother's breast pad was removed from her nursing bra and placed near her newborn's face, baby turned toward it, while ignoring breast pads from other mothers. "This special scent recognition also holds true for mothers," write Dr. William Sears and Martha Sears. "Blindfolded mothers can identify their own baby's smell."

Most Babies

Mrs. Elizabeth Greenhille of Abbots Langley, Great Britain, is alleged to have produced thirty-nine children (thirty-two daughters, seven sons) in a record thirty-eight pregnancies.

The Case of the Disappearing Baby Penis

A mound of fat that typically develops around the base of a baby's penis is called the "pubic fat pad." It often covers the baby's penis, prompting excited mothers and fathers to telephone their pediatricians with the alarming news that their baby's penis has "disappeared."

"No, it's not gone," writes Dr. William Sears, a San Clemente, California, pediatrician. "It resides comfortably buried beneath mounds of fat. As your baby goes through the normal stretching and lengthening of his whole body, the mounds of baby fat melt away and the penis reappears. This curious relationship between fat and penis acts the same in circumcised or uncircumcised infants."

Oldest Mom

The oldest mother on record to have conceived naturally is Mrs. Ruth Alice Kistler of Portland, Oregon. She gave birth to a daughter, Suzan, of Glendale, California, on October 15, 1956, when she was fifty-seven years and 129 days old.

Fastest Babies

Fastest triplet birth goes to Bradly, Christopher, and Carmon, who were born naturally to Mrs. James E. Duck of Memphis, Tennessee, on March 21, 1977. The three siblings took a total of two minutes to make their appearances.

Trendiest Names

According to *Parenting* magazine, the most popular "new" name for girls is Brianna, followed by Kaitlin and Chelsea. The trendiest boy's name is Austin, followed by Cody and Conner.

Androgynous names are popular, too. Cameron, Dakota, and Dylan top the list.

Fetal Fingerprints

At the age of three months a fetus develops fingerprints.

But identical twins *don't* have identical fingerprints.

Crying for Milk

Baby's cries have a tangible effect on Mother—no, not headaches. A baby's cries can trigger lactation in Mother's breast.

Film-star Babies

Seventy percent of camcorder buyers say they plan to use the unit to film their babies.

It's a Reflex

Newborns exhibit all kinds of interesting reflexes that only last a few months. The Babinski reflex, for instance, is probably one of the most entertaining. Tickle the sole of baby's foot, and the toes fan out while the foot twists in. But the show doesn't last long; between six and nine months this reflex drops out.

Talented Babies

Babies can breathe and swallow at the same time, an impossible feat for adults. This is a particularly handy talent that allows babies to breast-feed with maximum efficiency.

Who Brought the Stork?

Who created the tale that newborns are delivered by the stork? According to *The Book of Answers*, it was the ancient Scandinavians. The legend grew from their observations that storks are monogamous, treat their kin gently, and nest in chimneys. The myth, however, did not gain broad acceptance until the nineteenth century, when Danish writer Hans Christian Andersen popularized it in his fairy tales.

Most Popular Baby Months

According to the National Center for Health Statistics, July, August, and September are peak months for delivery in the United States, which means the most popular months for conception are November, December, and January.

How Much Does That Bundle of Joy in the Window Cost?

It depends on where you live. Having a baby can be an expensive proposition, but just how expensive depends a lot on geography. At the time of this writing, the cheapest place to have a baby is in the North Central United States, where the average cost for a vaginal delivery is $6,223, including physician and hospital.

The most expensive place is the Northeast, where the cost is about 27 percent higher—$8,541 for a vaginal delivery; $14,716 for a C-section.

Don't Be Cross If Your Baby Is Cross-eyed

Newborns often have crossed or wandering eyes because the muscles that control their eye movements are not yet coordinated. They also have extra folds of skin at the inner corners of their eyes that make baby *appear* cross-eyed.

Breast-Feeding Works Up a Thirst

It's common for a mother to become thirsty while breast-feeding her baby, because of the loss of fluids. Therefore, experts recommend that you drink at least eight 8-ounce glasses of water per day. The more water you drink, the more milk you'll produce.

22

Grow, Baby, Grow

I t's often said that kids "shoot up" because they grow so fast. This is especially true in the first two years, when the average child increases his birth length by 75 percent, and he's one fifth as heavy as he will be at eighteen years. The average child will double his birth length in four years.

Fat-free Babies?

A 1992 study conducted at the University of California at Davis found that breast-fed babies are leaner than formula-fed infants during the first two years of life.

Experts recommend delaying the introduction of solids until four to six months to lessen the risk of obesity.

Sensitive Babies

The sense of touch, one of the first senses to develop, has been detected in human embryos less than eight weeks old.

Relax, Mom! It's Good for You—and Your Baby

Recent studies have indicated that tension and stress can hamper a pregnant woman's ability to absorb nourishment. Consequently, her baby may be irritable, hyperactive, or of low birth weight.

Fearless Babies

Like puppies, kittens, and other young animals, babies have no instinctual fear of heights—another reason why they have to be watched so closely.

Rub Baby the <u>Right</u> Way

Rubbing gently between a drowsy baby's eyes will help him to fall asleep.

Just Your Average Baby

The average newborn weighs about seven and a half pounds and is twenty inches long. Boys tend to be slightly heavier than girls at birth.

Number-one Baby

First babies tend to be smaller than their future siblings.

Right on Schedule

Up to three weeks early or two weeks late, a baby is considered to be "at term."

A Little off Schedule

Eleven percent of babies were premature and 9.5 percent were postmature, according to a recent survey.

No Place like Home

Only about 3 percent of all births take place at home. However, before the 1920s, most births occurred at home with the help of a midwife. Only the very rich or very poor had hospital births.

High-tech Babies

About one thousand sets of triplets are born each year in the United States. Multiple births—twins, triplets, etc. —have more than doubled in the last twenty years. Technological advancements, experts claim, are a big part of the reason. New fertility drugs often increase the likelihood of multiple births.

Also, the fact that women are having babies later increases the chance of a multiple birth.

A Word about Babies

The average number of intelligible words parents can expect from babies is ten words for fifteen-month-olds; fifty words for eighteen-month-olds; and twenty-five to 400 words for two-year-olds. For three-year-olds it's about one thousand.

What's the Formula?

According to many experts, formula-fed babies are generally constipated more often than those who are breast-fed.

You Gotta Crawl Before You Can Walk

The average crawling age is between seven and ten months.

Walk This Way

Most babies learn to walk between twelve and fourteen months, but some learn as early as seven and eight months.

Generally, girls learn to walk and talk earlier than boys.

Now I Can Read My Own Stories

Many children of any age enjoy being read to, but most children learn to read around the age of six.

Big Girls, Big Boys

Most babies—boys and girls—double their birth weight in the first five months.

Bigger, Not Necessarily Better

According to Dr. Miriam Stoppard, author of *The Complete Baby and Child*, breast size has little to do with lactation. "Milk," writes Dr. Stoppard, "is produced in glands that are deeply buried in the breast, not in the fatty tissue, so breast size is no indication of how much milk you can produce; even small breasts are perfectly adequate milk producers."

Here's a Box of Crayons, but <u>Please</u> Stay Away from the Walls

It's no secret that kids love to color. American children spend about 6.3 billion hours a year coloring.

Barefoot Babies in the Park

It's easier for babies to walk barefoot than it is for them to walk in socks or shoes. Socks or shoes make them slip and slide, while bare feet give them a better grip on the ground. This traction helps to increase their walking skill and confidence.

What *Is* a Birthmark Anyway?

Birthmarks are nothing more than a cluster of blood vessels under the skin. They're also harmless and painless.

And Now I Lay Baby Down to Sleep

Recent studies have shown that for the first three months of your baby's life, it's best to lay baby on her back. Babies who sleep on their stomach are at a greater risk of SIDS—sudden infant death syndrome—than those put to bed on their back.

Shy Baby

Babies have an innate fear of strangers. Even the most outgoing baby will run and hide, withdraw, or even cry, when a stranger approaches. Unfamiliar surroundings have a similar effect on baby. Experts say, however, that this behavior is normal.

Head-banging Babies

It's not uncommon for babies to gently thump their heads against the mattress, crib, or wall. This behavior, once thought to be neurotic, is now understood to be a natural way for babies to release tension and produce a soothing rhythm that helps them fall asleep. Some babies thump their chest like Tarzan or hit themselves in the face. While this behavior can be unsettling to observing parents, in most cases, doctors say, it's not a cause for concern.

Thumbs Up for Thumb-sucking Babies

Children suck a finger or a thumb because it soothes them. Studies show that over half of all children do this in early childhood. Doctors say that this practice need not be discouraged until a child is about four or five years. At that age, thumb sucking can damage teeth, but generally, by that time, kids stop anyway, usually as a result of peer pressure.

No Smoking, Please

An estimated 25 percent of women in the United States smoke throughout pregnancy. The U.S. Public Health Service estimates that if no pregnant women smoked, infant deaths would be reduced by 10 percent.

Weight Loss Baby-style

Babies usually lose one tenth of their body weight in about the first five days of life. This quick weight loss is mostly the result of a reduction in body fluid.

But during baby's first year, she'll triple her birth weight.

Studly Babies

Parents are sometimes alarmed and surprised by their baby's spontaneous erection during bathing or changing. Although at this stage of development this is more of a reflex than a sexual response, baby's genitals are sensitive. Experts say that this is normal and that the best way for parents to react is matter-of-factly. This will help prevent your baby from developing a sense of shame about his body and genitals.

Worlds Apart

Worldwide, about 80 percent of the population does not practice circumcision.

The Working World

Sixty-five percent of women work throughout the entire nine months of their pregnancy.

Fifty-three percent of mothers head back to work before their baby's first birthday.

Colorful Babies

Babies of all races are bright pink or red at birth. After a few days, sometimes after only a few hours, their skin will start to show its true color. According to *American Baby* magazine, "bluish hands and feet are not uncommon in newborns, and when baby cries, her skin may turn purplish or red."

It's common, too, for newborns to have skin irritations. Spots, blotches, and red marks appear in the first few days, but at around three weeks of age the skin adapts and the markings disappear.

Cry, Baby, Cry II

During the first week of life, a normal baby spends about half his waking hours crying.

That's a lot of crying, but most babies cry tearlessly until they are one month old. At this age the lacrimal glands begin to mature and are able to produce real tears.

Chubby Babies, Chubby Adults?

If you think your baby is too fat, wait a minute before you enroll her in an aerobics class. According to the latest research, there's very little connection between an obese baby and an obese adult.

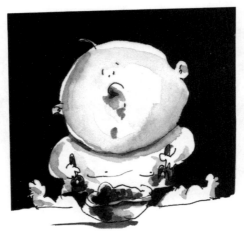

A Baby with Bite

Typically, babies start to get their teeth between six and nine months of age, most often around the seventh month.

Breast-feeding Can "Nourish" Mom Too

Medical evidence shows that breast-feeding helps mother's uterus contract faster after the birth of her baby. It also helps control her weight. One recent study found that the incidence of breast cancer among women who have nursed is lower.

Food Fight

A new study that appeared in *The Journal of Pediatrics* shows that parents' attitude toward food plays as much of a role in the weight of their baby as the food itself. Excessive control of food by parents may make a child more likely to be fat. The study found that of the children it profiled, ranging from ages three to five years, those with the most body fat had parents who were preoccupied with diet—theirs as well as their babies'.

Don't Put That in Your Mouth!

Babies seem to put everything in their little mouths, everything from toys to rattles to blankets. The reason for this is that, at least at first, the mouth is the baby's primary sense organ. It's the only means she has to get to know the world until she learns to use her whole body and the rest of her senses to discover her environment.

Off to See the Doctor . . .
Again

Healthy babies should be seen by their pediatrician at least six times during the first year of life, recommends the Committee of Psychosocial Aspects of Child and Family Health of the American Academy of Pediatrics.

Every Breath You Take

A newborn's breathing and heart rates are twice as fast as an adult's.

Day for Night

I nfants usually have one long rest period, but it's not necessarily at night.